"…Jennifer Maritza McCauley
so, so fantastic…"
—Joanna C. Valente, *Luna Luna*

"…No matter which genre you want to prowl, [McCauley's]
there, at home and decidedly not with words whose kinship
has been thrust upon them, and whose new reals she has
taken up the mantle of honoring and ameliorating. How
fortunate we are that our recognition of discomfort and pain
in constant acclimation is softened by [McCauley's] curiosity
and graciousness with even the prickliest of it. How much
better suited we are, when we listen, to being the citizens of
the future we need now to be…"
—Marc McKee, host of the Next Weather Series and
author of *Fuse* (Black Lawrence Press, 2011) and
Bewilderness (Black Lawrence Press, 2014.)

"…McCauley gives her characters the ability to express
metaphor and feeling in their conversations even as she uses
metaphor in her descriptive prose…"
—Anne Graue, *New Pages*

"…No matter the genre—[McCauley] uses rhythm and
voice to create music from words…"
—Aarik Danielsen, *Columbia Daily Tribune*

ACKNOWLEDGMENTS

"Loriella is Dead," "Brother Invisible." *Puerto del Sol*.
("Loriella is Dead" republished on Academy of American Poets.org)

"When Trying to Return Home." *Aspasiology*.

"Baby Dolls." *The Los Angeles Review*.

"La Vida Es Un Carnival Celia Sings at the Underground Mall." *The Boiler*.

"What Joy" "Some Advice" *Queen Mob's Tea House*.

"When They Say Stop Speaking Ghetto" "Baila, Papi" "My Black Girl" "Casting Call."
Luna Luna.

"Mulatto-ed." *The Feminist Wire*.

"The Girl We Forgot." *Hermeneutic Chaos*.

"A Good Song." *LED Publishing/Partial Press*.

"Old Blood." *Split This Rock/The Quarry: Poem of the Week*

"An End." *Columbia Journal*.

"From the Ghosts of Dead Boy Street." *For Harriet*.

"The Other Saints of New Orleans." *Deep South Magazine*.

"Summer of Screens" "40 Ways to Avoid Sexual Assault." *Public Pool*.

"But There is Also Rosa." *Passages North*.

"Summer Love, On Sidewalks," "The Girls Who Get Off the City Bus," "We Are
Always at Somebody's Party." *Literary Orphans*.

"Dear HomePlace" (originally published as "American Sacrileges.") *Connotation Press*.

SCAR ON / SCAR OFF

SCAR ON / SCAR OFF

ISBN: 978-0-9991152-0-6
Library Of Congress data available on request.

First paperback edition published by Stalking Horse Press, October 2017

www.stalkinghorsepress.com

Design by James Reich
Cover Photograph by Sylvain Reygaerts

Stalking Horse Press
Santa Fe, New Mexico

Stalking Horse Press requests that authors designate a nonprofit, charitable, or humanitarian organization to receive a portion of revenue from the sales of each title.

JENNIFER MARITZA MCCAULEY

SCAR ON / SCAR OFF

STALKING HORSE PRESS
SANTA FE, NEW MEXICO

CONTENTS...

ONE (I)

TWO (WE)

THREE (US)

Have you ever been hurt and the place tries to heal a bit,
and you just pull the scar off of it over and over again?
—Rosa Parks

The women I am from are wild: beautiful
This is what I know
When Lucille died, I tell my grand daughter
We are like Lucille trouble in the waters can't kill us
—Monica A. Hand

For Abbito, Sonia, Jerry and Timmy, as all things always are.

ONE

(I)

LORIELLA IS DEAD

Yesterday Loriella choke-cried into my phone,
saying we black gals got to stick together, hip to hip
since the world is a leech sucking at our night
necks, and I said girlIhearyou and I could hear
her voice cleaving clean down the center and
I remembered this was the girl who kicked a blackboy
down the stairs of Litchfield Towers, and burned my books
in the dorm yard when I told her I couldn't love her like that—
with all-the-time love, with only-her love

and she said give me sweet words then and I said what sort
and she burned my books again, the next night, on the dormhall yard
and told me my skin was the wrong kind of tawny,
that I was too soft-voiced to be a real black girl, that
everything I said was too long for listening.

Yesterday, she was talking and her voice got soaked with
ghosts, of men who sexed her bad and women who
gave her lies of love, and I remembered the other nights
she called me, when we were young and tighter-skinned, and
she talked about firearms and gun barrels and her
Auntie's arm-burns and she said she'd never
do what her Auntie did though she thinks about
what it'd be like to go away, with no man or woman draining her
dead, to go away by her own hands like Auntie did that
night when we were playing Scrabble on the dormhall
floor and she got the call that said Auntie is dead
Auntie left the room.

Yesterday, Loriella thanked me for love, said I was okay and
she knows her head is cut-up and we agreed that every
head is cut-up and every little black girl head is a little
tired and today her Mama calls me and says

Loriella is dead, and asks me what I said to her and
I said nothing, just that we black girls got to stick together
hip to hip, heart to heart, and her Mama says
how come you didn't try any kind of talk to make
My Girl live and I listen to fat air on the phone and her Mama's
cold cries, and I imagine Loriella's neck, life-broken, on the floor.
I think of its fleshy folds and clavicle, her pink mouth,
how it pursed and pouted and spoke fear and I think of what

I said every day when we were young: What do you want
me to tell you? and how I wondered what
words could do. I tell her Mama that, as
I choke-cry, "What could words have done?"

BROTHER INVISIBLE

When Timmy came out
he was bedsheet-white and Mami
thought, maybe he will look like me, but then
his skin got *pan*-colored and toasted dark,
and now he is blacker than our black Daddy.

If you see Timmy now, he dances
like the *negritos* in the clubs that find me
when I'm standing alone, but he is better
than all the boys, and Mami knows this
and she is glad.

When Blessed came out, he was red and
never changed colors. His eyes were knit-shut
and his foot-heels didn't twitch and Mami
said he will never look like any of us, and she
cried when they put Blessed's red body in a little box
and she said he will never look like anything and
she is right.

Sometimes, I imagine my ghost brother, what his
color would look like in the light if he were not
red or in a box. I wonder if he would dance in clubs
like the darkboys who talk to me when I stand
alone or if he would get fat or long-boned or

what name he would pick for me when we
are shoving shoulders, or playing pick-up
or waiting for Mami to take us home, and I

wonder what it would be like to have
a new-colored brother call out my name
and say, *let's go home.*

WHEN TRYING TO RETURN HOME

In the morning, I leave a *panadería* on SW 137th
and a Miami browngirl sees my face
and says *de dónde eres Miami* or Not?
And I say Not, because I live in this blue city now
but she means where are your parents from
and I tell her I have a Daddy who is Lou-born
and coal-dark and looks like me and I have a Mami
who is from Puerto Rico and looks like the *trigueña*
in front of us who is buying piraguas for her yellow children.

The browngirl says *eres Latina* at least, and I say at least
in English. I look down at my skin, which is black, but
smells blue by the shores of Biscayne. She thinks my skin could
speak Spanish, *a los menos*. I want to tell the browngirl I was not born
by ocean rims or white-scuffed waves. I was not born
beside browngirls who speak Miami's itchy Spanish. I was born
where my culture rarely bloomed—amongst Northern steel-dust and
dead skies, where my two-colored parents stuck out at any
Pittsburgh party. I want to tell her, I would love to be the type of girl
that says *soy de* Somewhere and everyone says, "Girl, I see"
or "you're *una de las nuestras*"
or "you belong."

I want to tell her, you are right, in this blue city, I look like everybody
and everybody looks like me, and this is the thing I've always wanted:
to be in a crowd where nobody remembers my skin. I've wanted
this when I was a child, amongst grey buildings and steel-dust
where they called me unloved and weird-colored but here, *mija*,
I smell like blue and people who look like Mami can say funny
things like at least, at least.

Instead, I smile at the browngirl and she does not smile back.
Instead she says, in Spanish: If you are Latina, you should be so,
speak Spanish to me. And I say, in English: Yes, I could
but I am afraid, and she laughs in no language and judges me.

I want to tell her the history of my family-gods. They are rainforest-hot,
cropland-warm, dark with every-colored skin. They have mouths
that sound like all kinds of countries. I want to tell her these gods
live wild and holy in me, in white and blue cities where my skin
is remembered or forgotten, in cities where I am always one thing, or
from anywhere.

I want to tell the browngirl this while she turns and walks off.
I want to tell her that when she came to me, thinking I was hers
in that moment we were together,

at least.

BABY DOLLS

My brother is little, black-skinned, and sleeping deep in a cloud-colored bassinet. I am also little and black, but longer-limbed, four-years old with plaits greased tight by Mami's yellow fingers. It is mid-September but the living room growls with fanged heat. Mami is downstairs soaking pigeon peas and Abuela is with me, laughing at *luchadores* on television. The wrestlers glow with sweat and slippery oil; they twist, curl and snap in grotesque shapes. Abuela sips Coors and rocks Timmy idly. I watch my brother's slitted eyes, his waxy, fat-pocked skin. He looks doll-like but his humped belly is real and trembles under duck print cotton. Mami has told me *don't pick him up; he's not a toy* but I know this already. I know my brother is not a doll; he is a plushy seed that will bloom into my first real friend.

/

I am little, black and smiling, months before, in the corner of my nursery school's playroom. It is the end of the day and I build a Lincoln Log cabin alone. The girls and boys, all pink-colored, except for Kuja and Yi, are in friend-clusters, playing with T Rexes or Raggedy Annes or floppy ballerinas. Mami arrives early. She scans the playroom, walks about and inspects the doll-faces—the blue-eyed plastic babies with peach fuzz hair, the princesses with pinched-in waists. She looks at me and sees me: smiling, black, friendless. Mami's eyes get red and she licks her lips. She isn't happy and says so. Mami is not black, but she reads books every day on How to Raise a Black Child by Very Smart Black Scholars and she knows her black daughter should have the right dolls. Mami confronts Miss O'Donnell then, who is laughing with pig-tailed brunettes. Mami asks about the dolls first. She points at the toys, then Kuja and Yi, then me. Mami talks loud. Miss O'Donnell sighs and says we don't have that kind of budget to change things for three girls. The teacher does not know Daddy is an Important Black Man, and Mami names all the Important Men Daddy knows. The teacher blinks too many times; she is shrinking. Mami grabs my hand and we are gone.

The next week, new dolls come to my school. They are copper-faced like Kuja and oval-eyed like Yi and black like my father, with Daddy's sheepskin hair.

When Mami comes to fetch me, she looks to see how things have changed. She sees me: little, black, alone, and smiling in the corner, dreaming up adventures with different-colored dolls. Mami's face muscles get weak. She picks me up, and marches past the nursery school teacher. The nursery school teacher smirks when we leave.

In the car, Mami buckles me in. She sits in the driver's seat and slams her head against the car wheel. She is sobbing.

/

My brother is little, black, and still sleeping-deep, while Mami finishes the *gondules* downstairs. Abuela doesn't like the *luchadores* show anymore and she switches to *telenovelas*. She opens another can of Coors or "Special Soda," the kind of drink Daddy says I cannot have. I ask Abuela what she is drinking, if it is poison like Daddy says. Abuela laughs and hands me the can. She says something too-fast in Spanish and I don't understand her. I sip small, and my mouth burns fast. I shove the can back in Abuela's hands and run to the bathroom. I spit in the sink. My teeth are hot; my gums prickle. Daddy was right; it was bad stuff, and I'm going to die. I wonder if Abuela was trying to warn me in Spanish or poison me. Maybe Abuela was giving me a mean language test, and if I passed I'd officially be included on Mami's side of the family. If I failed, I didn't belong to Abuela or Mami. I had failed.

I am done spitting and I go to sit next to my grandmother on the couch. I shiver. Abuela smiles at me, then points at a blonde-haired *telenovela* actress on the screen. Abuela says her white face is *"pura y beautiful"* and she says something else loving I can't understand. I wonder if she'll ever speak of me with this kind of warmth in her mouth. I stand back up and look at my little brother, whose sweet face makes me better-feeling. I tell him I love him, just in case I won't be alive for much longer. My brother stares at me as if he knows me very well.

Abuela sees me and says, "Picking him up?" I tell her, Mami says Not To, and Abuela says a few more words in Spanish, then, "It will be cute." I look at Timmy and decide I will hug him one last time before the poison kicks in. I reach to lift my brother. Timmy is too heavy for my little girl arms. The bassinet lurches to the left. Abuela cries out and catches it; I am holding my brother who has tipped over, face first, his stomach smashed against the rim of the carriage. He is wailing and I am holding his chest. I cry too and Abuela is cussing and Mami shows up. She is horrified. Mami rushes forward and pries Timmy from my hands while Abuela holds the bassinet in place. I reach out, try to help, but Mami shouts something in Spanish, and I can't tell if she is yelling at me or Abuela, but I run away anyway. I don't want to see the faces of my family as they turn against me.

In my room, on my little girl bed, I press my face against the pillow and cry. I wonder how long it will take to die from Abuela's soda. I think I'll never see my brother again now, and my Mami, who probably doesn't love me anymore, thinks I have tried to hurt Baby Timmy. I won't play with him again. If I survive Abuela's soda, I will always be alone.

After the pillow gets damp from my little girl snot and tears, I look up. I see my dolls. They crowd my plaid comforter. They are the friends Mami bought for me so I will not be lonely. I look at these purchased friends: plastic cocoa girls with puffy braids, brown babies with wild hair, Latina-looking Barbies with ochre legs and wet black eyes. They stare at me, coldly. They are me-colored, dead-eyed, unreal.

WHAT JOY

today,
somebody said
you look so happy
it's almost
like you
have
nothing
inside
of you.

LA VIDA ES UN CARNIVAL CELIA CRUZ SINGS AT THE UNDERGROUND MALL

Life is the carnival:
Celia sings and asks me to salsa/shimmy-shimmy to the quick beat of *alegría*,
lightness and robust love. She tells me to stomp
and stamp on these floors with slick-edged boots.
She tells me to forget the things I remember about carnivals like
the strategic placement of pear cores and elephant
shit and the man who says youcan'tgoinyet, that man who says
kids

there is a line, a line, a line.

Es mas bello vivir cantando:
Celia sings on, and I suppose a sensitive artist could transform
the man in the trashbag suit yowling for a quarter or a coupon,
into some sort of god. Instead, I push shoulders and think

go, go, go, go, go, go go.

We are the animals:
Women with earrings hooped like circus rings, ladies with horse snouts
neighing at the sound of sale. Teens with rectangle tongues out, licking
up pink cream and sugardust. A wail as bad as old blues rips out
of panhandler with a kettle-shaped ass who has fallen

bottom first.

I'd know this scene anywhere:
The festival of faces, the fat mink hair tossed
atop thin-boned skulls, the jelly walk of men
with doughnut flakes wedged into regal mustaches.
The skip and shuffle of rough-heeled sneakers, the teeny
shirts boasting drawings of Diego, Barney, Dora or a white
cardcatcher with a Japanese name. The squeaks
on tiles, the mid-back pushes, the elbow shoves;
the gravel pants of folks who want to rush forward.

I am with them, always.

TWO

(WE)

THE GIRLS WHO GET OFF THE CITY BUS

There are babies in our bodies.

We look heavy but our eyes are light-stuffed. We get off the 71A, bound by elbow and hip, and we get off laughing.

Passersby guess our ages. We know we are too-young. We know what it means to have bellies egg-shaped like this, with skin blue-dark like this. We think about tucking our heads down, but we don't. We flick our mouths up. We laugh about some boy acting tricky. We catch dying snowflakes with our bottom gum. We imagine ourselves growing, fatter and wider, until there's nothing left on these streets but our enormous stomachs and our hot new-Mama-love.

With these black bodies, big as God and filled with all kinds of delicate weather, we are happy that we can create something as beautiful as life.

WHEN THEY SAY STOP SPEAKING GHETTO

I am a rebel language,

the wild bloodroot of
ancestral line.

I ain't gonna speak in
your cusses nor *cursivos,*
oye:

this talk
ain't school-taught,

it's ready for a gotdamn
brawl.

whatchu 'fraidofman
tienesmiedo,'mano?

what horrors could
possibly come from
these dumb,
dagger-
words?

SUMMER LOVE, ON SIDEWALKS

I ain't checkin' you.

You callin' out to me from across 17th and Ashberry but you callin' too-sweet. I don't say nothing. I just show you my shoulder and turn to my half-circle of girls. They throw you a third finger and wiggle their double-drop earrings. You ain't checkin' them. You stampin' your workboots, brushin' your face with your palm-heels, slappin' your thighs, and shouting out your nothing-love.

You singin', "Hey, baby! Stop actin' tricky! Come over, come over! I been looking at you, thinking you the one!"

My girls and me, we got a bus to catch. I ain't missing my connection to the little job I got 'cause you want to play my shapes. My girls and me, we been hearing you and your boys talkin' about girl-shapes, about our smooth and tight places, about the hips you want to drum, the nipples you want to pluck, the bought-hair you want to tug and strum. Boys like you are always trying to warm us up with your hot dreams. We ain't checkin' you. We remember when a boy like you came and snatched one of our girls, last winter. We saw you buying her mint-cream cones, saw you scoopin' summer season into her mouth. We saw you kissing her shy cheekbone, heard your *"siempres"* and *"trust'ames."* We remember how you loved our girl foul, then threw her back, hollowed out and soul-bruised. We remember you blamed her, said she was too thin-chested and fat-legged, while you were switching your eyes at some other gal's wobbling ass.

Our Mamas and Tias been warning us about you since we were babies. They been saying, "Careful, careful, and *cuidate, cuidate, mija*" since we first pulled on satin dresses and pledged to be princesses. They loved boys that gave nothing-love too, and that bad love got them fat with baby or red in the mind.

So when the bus pulls up and you still shouting my name, saying, "Yes, yes, you the one, you the one I want," I ain't checkin' you. I ain't noticing the waves and rolls of your night hair, not your quick flash of dimple or slick, small teeth. No, I ain't checking you. Not me. But my girl on the left, she ain't gettin' on the bus with us. She cutting her eyes at us, then looking at you. Now you calling her name. We claw for her, but she taking off across the street. We crying for her, but she followin' the sound of your ugly voice instead.

THE GIRL WE FORGOT

Don't talk about my life: carved red on Abeje's wrist-bones, cursive curls like Mrs. Zeze taught her in the special kids class. Abeje was private: she told us, I'm a private girl.

The day before she died, my friend and I saw Abeje, big-bellied, wandering 'round the schoolhall after sixth period. Abeje was saying things like "I got a bad stomach and hate, got my Daddy too much around," then she got dark-eyed and went to the bathroom and Mrs. Zeze had to carry her away.

We knew Abeje. She lived with her Daddy in Lavender Flats, room #31, right below our family. We remembered her Daddy's beast-groan, her fear of pushing out sin or her father's chunky blood. We knew these things about Abeje, but her life scared us. We were little girls, then, afraid of everything.

We stamped by her corpse on the way out of Lavender Flats the next day, that body: oaken and shining, tucked in a tangle of sweetspire. We watched Important People shove oldfolk shoulders and rose-dotted waists. We punctured the halo of tenants, and they were pointing: at the dead blackgirl with the egg-stomach, her back bent like a downspout. The crowdfolks said Abeje tipped off the roof on her own. She flew. Some said her death was pretty to watch, if you didn't know her.

Then, sirens spun and sang, and her Daddy rushed in, stocking-footed, in love an hour too late. We kept walking and focused instead on soft thoughts: our lunchtime lunches in tin boxes, Mama-made. We thought about our butter cakes and naked yams, and ignored the red on Abeje's knees and dress-pleats.

When we came home that night, our parents asked us what we knew about the girl from #31. We said, "Not much." They asked what we saw and we said nothing to tell, and they asked us if Abeje was our friend. We lied and said yes, knowing we didn't like talking to that private girl, because we were still little, afraid of everything.

Our parents hugged our corduroy bodies. They said, "We're here to talk, please do," as if they were worried about how we would be raised. We said, don't worry none and we remembered Abeje's flattened belly and white pupils. We remembered her banged up body again and we threw up later, while our parents were sleeping.

We were little girls, then, becoming private.

WE ARE ALWAYS AT SOMEBODY'S PARTY

Everyone is talking about Big Topics at the summer gala. I hear them choking on seas and continents.

They are talking about women-pain, baby corpses, and dusky bodies shot from chest to soul. They count the colors of the people in the room and their voices turn red.

Somebody asks how I feel about Big Topics. I say nothing. I have seen bloody babies; I have felt woman-pain. I've seen the clouds in a dead man's pupils. I am one of the dark colors they mention. Nobody in the room has my skin. Still, one of their Big Topics is what to do with people like me.

Somebody I know says my name, asks what I think. The others turn to me and I am glad. I have all sorts of stories to tell. My stories aren't always about Big Topics.

I open my mouth. When I speak, they smile. They will quote me at other summer galas. They will say "I know this sort of person…she would know about a thing like this…because she's one of them…" They will say I am their friend and they will look stout-hearted and informed. They will not invite me to supper at their homes.

They watch my mouth move for a little longer, then cut me off.
I am shrinking.

They are speaking, again. I watch them choke down oceans, gnaw on fat slabs of countries. I watch their mouths grow until they are too-huge and too-dark. I wonder if these mouths will be large enough to devour me someday.

MULATTO-ED

Our friends are talking about our babies, but we haven't got to the loving part yet.

They are looking at our skin, yours: burnt bread-colored because your parents are Japanese and Spanish and Jewish. Mine, tea-tawny, because my Mami and Daddy are Deep South and Bori-brown. Our friends show us happy teeth. They imagine our fictional babies and call them omni-racial; they talk about how we could count the colors divided between us. My *morena* coppers and coal-blacks, your Euro-whites, gypsy tans and Japanese olives. They talk about how our genes will mix and blush, that we'll produce a new kind of good that comes out smiling and gap-toothed and blended.

They are saying we could create some post-racial rainbow because that's what we need now, two nice people like you, who represent what has been neglected. Your children could make the world new and better. We don't say anything. We laugh but don't smile. We've never seen teeth shine with that kind of bright. When we were growing up, folks of all colors pointed at us and said, "Tell us where you're from," or "You are this thing" and "I hate you" and they gave us labels and we decided, after time, those folks didn't know a thing. We have never seen these hopeful faces, aimed at us before.

Really, you and I are brown fictions. We are fistfuls of colors that bear upon and burden us, but our parents shouldered the pain of all those colors, when they grew up, when they got to loving. We are young and only speak our parents' language, sometimes. We don't know how cultures should behave. We don't think about the eye-length or nose-shapes of our babies. We don't think about what we represent together or how to fix the post-racial lie, or how we can stop the pain pulsing in our bristling cultures because we are still deciding if we should love, and how.

/

You, me, and our friends are at your Oto-san's bar on Steeple Street, the bar he bought with his Turkish friend Micky. I am on vacation from school in the

South, and you live here in New London, always. We have been in love for three months, and that's not enough yet.

Our friends are tittering and drinking vodka on the red plush couches in the front of this little joint. You have to set up the sound system for the DJs who are coming in. I follow you.

In the backroom, our mouths kick out half-phrases of hope. We tug at the edges of love-words, pluck out impossible futures from bar-smoke. What if you lived here and I lived there, or you were from this family and I was from that. When can we make this happen, should we, why do you like what you like, why do you say things the way you do, do we match, you can be mean and I can be mean. You are lovely, I think I am too. We are broken, and have been broken, should we break each other again with this kind of love…

Meanwhile, the music minds us. Silk-strewn jazz, unwinds underneath pops of thin instrument. A woman cries a song about a man who will never leave his dead city. We are talking about the little things tucked in the sound that remind us of our parents. I find a fat blue funk, rippling under the bass. I call the Thing soul-black or *sabor*-rich, because the histories in my skin perk up when they hear a Mami or Mama-drum. You are saying something about how you wouldn't call sound culture, because when it dribbles thin out of the speakers it has no history nor color. You said you learned that when you saw your cousin spin "Superfreak" in too-bright Todai clubs, or when your students moonwalked in Majorca, or when you translated lyrics for your *primo* in Madrid who could out-rap Outkast. You said: everybody is eventually going to look like one thing and who cares what that looks like.

I'm saying *nah* and about to say something about Harlem history or *bomba* hips and the power of difference but your mouth hushes me. When we go back to see our friends, they see our hands clutched. They whistle. You order a second round, and we drink whisky and coke too-fast. Our friends grin, their grins are screaming.

/

There are other things we think about. We find them more important. They are more important than our babies, or even where we live now. We wonder:

what happens when the lightning in our teeth gets lonely. What happens when I can't see the smooth lines of your body or your voice gets too sharp-tipped, cold-edged. You wonder what happens when I stop acting soft, when I become a full woman with new-feeling, weary flesh. The sort of woman who might go anywhere, become anyone. We wonder if we can make it past the month. The month after. Past the next year. As they talk, we realize our clasped-together hands are negotiating future. We think that this part, the negotiation, is its own kind of future.

FROM THE INTERRACIAL DATING PEANUT GALLERY

I fall in love with Asianboys all the time.
I fall in love with whiteboys all the time.
I fall in love with Latinboys all the time.
I fall in love with blackboys all the time.

hehe: babygotyellowfever
hooo: thatsomeselloutlove
whoa: tamalegotchu?
goodgood, you catch 'em

blackgirl. but for your
life,
> *not the scary*
> *kind?*

A GOOD SONG

Look at this damn night:
I don't like it.

This night's all purple and pickled
with the same stars we been
seein' since we was babies,
and those stars are still talkin'
light to us, but nobody wants to
look up anymore.

This air's hanging too-heavy
with all our fastlife troubles and
here, at this party,
we prattlin' about new pains and
kiddie-fears and everything we say
is itchy and sticky and empty,
and nobody's listening to nobody,
we just spoutin' nothing-noise.
Yeah, everybody is angry and cawing
and hungry and nobody ate nothin'
all day but people.

I say, we need a good song.
Just a nice cut to dance to,
I say, a good song could cure
somethin'.

Yeah, we need a sweet swell of prayer
kicked into life by whatever that kid
on the pianoseat's gonna teach us
after his fingers bang up
the yellow teeth of his Steinway.

Now here he go. Now, everybody's
changin' their mind 'bout their
sad talk, now they leapin' up.
Seesee: look how everybody moves
and forgets, how we toss it all
once we get a plink and pluck,
a little pang and pow of good music,
see how this pianokid's
whippin' our hips into coil, how
he's makin' our legs
fling. See how
how he got our hands
to wriggle, jiggle, wake?

And now we've transformed:
our hair's sweat-wet,
our mouths are open with
joy and jargon,
and nobody remembers
a damn thing we was mewlin'
'bout.

See?
Now our faces are
soppin' up all that
purple sky
and we tellin' the kid on
the pianoseat to keep playing them
good songs until his fingers hurt
and our brains and bodies
are happily
wrung out.

BAILA, PAPI

Tonight in this Florida city,
while watching you
dance, I desperately,
want to worship you
like a girl in
pew. I want to tell you:
te quiero, te quiero
mi Papi bonito.

Hey, Pretty Papi,
you're a hot little light, ain't you,
a flat bed of water-skin. Look at you,
angel kid, you're a rain-wet
street after squall. Ay,
slick-bodied boy, Ima call you
mi empanada, stuffed to bursting with all
kinds of spicy, secret things.

'Bet you think I'm talkin' 'bout your hip-bones,
yeah, I know the whole world want to
lick them clean and so do I.
But for me, in these frothy times,
I see your eyes before your stomach-ripples,
and those eyes are fearsome as fire;
they got prophet-power.

Kid, I'm saying you're *sabor* pulsing, you're a tree that summer
'canes can't shake down. I'm saying you eye a mean day
and grip it fierce, punch it to ash and stone.
I'm saying if I got little shadows gobbling up
my road-bruised shoes, you gonna show me
how to stamp on them ghost-shapes 'til
whole world thinks I'm dancing.

And ain't you always dancing, sweet thang?

Oye, tonight, Ima tell you I love you, Papi.
And this little *negra* me is thinkin'
let's shiver and pump 'til we're loose-brained,
'til we're strong with shaking.
'til' we're so wicked
any devil would call us wild.

Oye, let's be mean as God.

Yeah, tonight, listen:
te quiero, Papi.
Sabes, when you movin' sexy
on that heartbeat floor,
you showin' us all the way
to some new kind of
heaven.

CASTING CALL

There is a casting call for
a rap video that says only cute
white and Latina girls acceptable,
and I want to show up with my Blatina-black
self speaking slanty Spanish. I'll take my pal Sumie
who is Armenian and Japanese,
and my girl Q who is German, trans, and Italian
as fuck, and we'll march on into wherever
we need to go and we'll be snapping. We'll be
jigging 'fore we get thrown out, we'll
be showing all our skin off.

They should see that:
us cute girls obeying that casting call
on an American
technicality, us
actin' so good,
lookin' all kinds of ways
like they won't
believe.

FROM THE GHOSTS OF DEAD BOY STREET

You don't know me. I've been ghosting here longer than your history remembers. My blood is patterned on the soil underneath your un-swept cement. You don't know that, nah, you treat my body like its devil-black, like it's soft to time. You've never seen my body as it is, bountiful, blazing, bronzed by God.

I'll tell you what my body ain't. My body ain't a thing to be tucked, blue and swollen under a scramble of snow. My body ain't a thing to be found. Nobody should have to see my little boy picture on the mid-day news. Nobody should have to remember whether I liked Doublemint or Bazooka, whether I chewed on cigarette tips or wore my jeans with a leather belt. My body is not a thing to be tossed or treated. It's a thing made to squeeze a Mama-waist or to snatch up tamarindo or to just run out running, alive.

I'll tell you this:

You cannot stuff this life in a house. You cannot manacle this life, or hurl it into a little shadowed room. My spirit is steaming up, through sidewalk cracks and haygrass, through the high roofs of corner markets. Before you came for me, you should have known this too:

If you take this body, this spirit ain't goin' float up to God and forget you. Nah, my spirit is huffing, puffing, hurting your glass; it's sleeping sweet in your daughter's bed. See? It's breathing.

This is a warning: this dead boy spirit can breathe, breathe, breathe.

WHILE VIEWING THE 2016 PRESIDENTIAL EXIT POLLS

We're trying to trust you
so badly, but listen:
now, when we swim through your
throbbing crowds
dressed in our age-old
different-skin,
we cannot
tell if we are
wading through
a familiar
tide, or
cutting through
waves of
white sheets.

OLD BLOOD

Before they tell us how to look
at our kilt brothers' bodies:

Tell them we already know how to see 'em.
Tell them we been mournin' bullet-warmed
blood long before they told us: now this is how
you interpret a death

Tell them we grew up learning how to
Dodgeshouthithurtlovegetquietbloodymove
Tell them we grew up learning how to run.

Tell them we been smearing our brothers'
dark wet stuff on our berry-black cheeks
long before those folks was mewlin' and baby-soft.

Tell them our blood belongs
to all of them too.
Tell them to look at our wounds, still
hot and wide-open:

damn it, just
look look look

look

THREE
(US)

AN END

I am afraid to die, my oldman client tells me. He says this while sipping a hot beer we snuck into the Oakmont hospice house. We are in his room and we stare out of his window, together. He points outside, at the traffic of river-wet loons as they shuffle up from shore. My oldman is afraid to die, and I have heard this sentence before, but never for real, only in cable dramas and HBO war films. My oldman reminds me his fear is a secret. He says I mustn't repeat this secret to his daughters or the other caregivers. Especially not the freckled girl who talks to him in baby voices, who pretends he's a teenager with untested bones.

My oldman says don'trepeatwhatIsaid again, and I nod, without cutting my eyes at his yellowed face. I don't know what to do with his secret but keep it, anyway. I don't understand what it is like to have full possession of your body but know you are weeks away from death. I don't know because I am young and nauseatingly alive. I don't understand what it is like to fear something so horrifying and universal and certain. I don't know how to swat his fears away. I am in my early twenties, and have been a caregiver for a year at this senior care center. My oldman and I bonded over John Wayne movies, Steelers games, the ritual of me wiping away half-stuck feces from his deflated ass cheeks while he shut his eyes in shame. He called me a "colored gal angel" or sometimes a "bitch who wouldn't give him more beer," and I would stay up all night waiting for him to fall asleep; I'd watch as he sputtered and wept and cried for his dead wife. I have told him few things about me and I have seen the worst parts of his lingering life.

Now, I've been told by doctors, his daughters, the giver with the freckled cheeks and my boss: your oldman is definitely going to die.

My oldman and I stare at the ducks hobbling away from foam-frilled banks. He says he has been feigning rosiness for his family. His lips hurt bad but he bends his mouth up. He wants to sleep but stays awake. He doesn't care about the Steelers anymore but he complains about them anyway. His daughters like to see him as he was: grumpy about ballgames, obsessive about sports-numbers and football stars. My oldman tells me he can't stand his daughters' face when he's quiet. Their chins are always quivering, their eyes night-dark. He has worked to death so they won't look that sad. He says he'd love to be who his daughters want him to be: a wrinkly sage who looks forward to his body-pain spiriting away. Who can't wait to see his beloved wife, who wants to hug Jesus Christ and snuggle with saints on a heavenly cloud.

My oldman tells me he'd like to be this wrinkly sage but he is so afraid of dying he can't sleep. This is why he is so tired during the day, because he can't sleep at night and this is why he wants to rest during the day instead of talking about Steelers scores. Because if he falls asleep and dies in the light, he'll be around busy folks, orange glares, me, his daughters. That way somebody might see what happened, might accurately tell the story of his end.

My oldman finishes his beer. He asks me what to do, as if I might know. Me, then: a twenty-two year old virgin who is saving my caregiving money so I can move to Miami for graduate school. Me, then: a baby-minded thing who only knows how to repeat what is told.

I say, shakily: You'll be okay and this is the worst answer because it is dumb and it is a lie. My oldman nods tiredly and looks out the window.

He bites the beer can and we say nothing.

Two weeks later my oldman dies in his sleep, during the day. His youngest daughter was picking up her kids at nursery school and I was picking up a new shift when it happened. My boss calls to tell me the news while I am driving to the Harmarville Target. She says: I called you because... I'm sorry to say this... but I already know why she's calling. We discuss the details of my oldman's death and the new, half-alive client I must care for tomorrow, who will die shortly, who is also probably afraid. My boss keeps talking and I say uhhuh and some other things before I slam my Focus into the car in front of me that is stopping for a red light.

I pull over and wait for the driver to get out. She climbs out of her Jeep carefully. I walk up to her, give her my information. I watch this woman scribble the superficial facts of my life on the back of a Burger King receipt. She is writing what I tell her: my car's make and model, my Daddy-given name, my address and phone number. All evidence of my short and stupid life. Underneath the red of Target storeface, I watch this woman record everything I tell her about me. She finishes quickly; I don't have much to say. She looks up, wondering if my body is shaken. It is not. I was young then, nauseatingly alive.

THE SUMMER OF SCREENS

i.

In Pittsburgh, Mami is in the kitchen pointing
at the news and yelling Puerto Rican
fuego-style at the announcer. She
says: *what does it matter if someone says what
they know if you know they don't care?*

ii.

It is summer, and I am black, in Thibodaux, alone.
An old friend calls me from Georgia
and her voice is red. She cries about bad sex and
lost love and her new life becomes my fault.
I hear how mad she is and it makes me mad,
just hearing the heat bake in her mouth
hundreds of miles away.

She proposes, after our voices have gotten high,
that perhaps our friendship is pure and real, and
this is why we are talking mean. She suggests
that the reason people yell is because they want to be
understood and, in love, you always want
your Other to feel as if she knows you, as if
you are deeply known.

She thinks this is why people screech at each other:
because they want to be understood, or known, and if
not known, remembered.

On television, a Democrat is slapping his hands
together and yelling *nonono*, and a Republican is hollering
thatsnottruenottruenottrue. They cannot see each other
but they can hear each other's bawdy voices. Us tv-watchers
can see their faces clearly, how their cheeks
pinken and blue.

There is a moment when the Democrat and Republican
both say something about love,
about loving America fierce,
but I almost missed it,
the love-part,
because it was tucked underneath spirals of hot note
and stinging sound.

iii.
On YouTube, Beyonce has tied up that
blonde weave we've been seeing for years
into tight braids that look like shadowed cornfields,
shining against her expensive scalp. She
is twitch-dancing, her soft-hard legs jerking
to the sound of pop and power, a beat
rehearsed to make us shout "yeah, girl, please!"

Beyonce isn't wearing white and she's not
having fun anymore. She wants you to know she won't
have as much white fun. On YouTube, she glowers
at me and descends into Katrina-water, while sitting
on top of a copcar she bought for this video.

In another video, Donald Trump calls my graduate school
by name and says it is full of little black people with little
white leaders, and he looks me in my eye and reminds me
I am one of the little black people he hates.
I click on Beyonce's video again because I know this dark
rich woman, in a game of theoreticals, loves me
far more than Donald Trump.

When I realize this, Beyonce is no longer glaring,
she's saying, "girl, we got this, I'm with you," and she is
glistening fine and smooth. Her royal black skin could be mine
but it isn't.
Her skin: as shiny as a money-coin.

When she sings ladiesgetinformation I start crying
and don't know why, because I know this is
a video and she has purchased all of our culture's
chilling symbols and will go back to a queen-home
I will never see. But when I see her skin like this: suddenly black
and toughly smooth on my small computer, she reminds me of who
I am. This summer I could be one of those Bey-lovin' blackfolks
worshipping my be-weaved goddess from the backrow of
a concert that costs half my rent. Maybe, before I go back to
my busted Ford, me and other blackgirls and boys might get lucky
enough to pass her security guards, to walk around the concert
copcars she owns, that we could never buy
for protection. I still, desperately,
want to getinformation.

I click off the video,
when she sings:
SLAY SLAY SLAY
SLAY SLAY SLAY

iv.
I'm back home up North and a rich blackgirl
I sort-of remember from my not-rich college, sees my skin
and asks me how many times I'm gonna use a black lives hashtag
today like she is asking me if I believe Jesusismy
personalsavior. I tell her, politely, I've used the hashtag
a bunch of times, and I've been out in these streets with
big ass signs since Trayvon and I've been a nigger since
I was childborn and been a nigger since. I show her the
receipts of my Black Protest Participation and Black Graduate
Education, and she does not remember me
but decides to like me, then.

She invites me to something she is leading but I'm already walking
to another black thing that doesn't make black folks
feel heathen-like, like Jesus is not their personal savior.
I think about turning around and telling her, girl, this

is not like inviting Jesus into your life as your
personal savior and by the way Jesus will not
rescue you in one moment, he will take his bloody
time to save you good and none of the whitefolks
you yelling at are gonna change their lives because
of how many times I use that hashtag.

I don't say anything because she and I are sewn by spirit
and skin. She and I know what it feels like to
see your brother's jaw smashed against a copcar hood or
to get pulled over on the way to your to-do 'hood
because a cop doesn't believe you live in a good place
and he gives you a $100 ticket for an air freshener because
he doesn't know what to charge you for, so he reaches in
and smells the plastic bags of trash in your car and says
girls like you hide drugs and don't live in good places,
so you watch him smell your trash.
She knows what we feel all feel like.
What black folk don't?
Why would I condemn her when Trump
is alive and trumpin'?
How much wokeness will cure memory?

But I should be
better.

I remember her, then:
she is the same person who came up to me six years ago
talking about sororities, with yellow weave long, lush
and crackling with power. She told you your kinky hair
need to get laid, you got that whitegirl ass. She's the same girl
who said that Chinese boy you with is whack,
you gotta drop him for a Mandigo.

Now, I answer the question sweetly and leave soft,
as if I'm saying Jesus has always been my personal savior,
as if I'm in the South and telling her God bless you, as if
I have to fight with the choir, instead of preach to it,

as if I have to prove to a narrow-eyed Christian
why Jesus really is my personal savior. But I'm
wondering, still:

Why do I have to explain
anything to my own choir?

v.

In Tennessee, I watch Alton Sterling
and Philando Castille die on my computer screen
because this is the kind of age I am
aging in. When I was a kid it'd take six hours
to download a bootleg episode of Rurouni
Kenshin on Real Player, when I was a kid
if some blackman died nobody remembered it, unless
he'd killed someone special or raped someone
in Wilkinsburg and maybe you'd get that two
minute clip of his dusty, wild-eyed mugshot and
he wouldn't get a name, he'd just be Wilkinsburg
Man Who Killed [Somebody] Then Killed Himself, and we knew
they were saying Man, but they'd say it with a slant, so we'd know
Wilkinsburg Man was somebody called Rashad or Trey,
and he looked like our black boyfriends,
who were good-hearted and preachers' sons
and still dodging cops. We'd know all the white folks
would think Wilkinsburg Man could be every
blackman, anywhere.

And we'd forget Wilkinsburg Man if he weren't famous,
because the news forgot about him halfway
through the story they were telling that was mostly
about how it was his fault.

Now, if I want to, I can watch a real blackman die on my shitty
Asus, I can watch a man heave and clutch his chest while the girl
who loves him watches and keeps the focus on his lovely, dying
face. This is the new digital age I live in, and I think,

now, haven't we come to some kind
of revolution.

I watch a man who looks like my little brother gasp for life
and I watch his dark body lose a battle against itself.
I am watching this, alone, in the Southest of Souths.

A white friend from Canada sends the video to me in an email,
as if I haven't seen it.

He writes, guilelessly:
"Whoa. What do you think about this?"

SOME ADVICE

He says you have it coming
because you smile
too-big at the Papis and gals and no matter
the meaning behind that smile, baby,
your joyful teeth are enough to
jail you in consequence.

He says whatever happens
when he releases me into the wet night
after a weird beer or somekinda wine
is my own fault, that I can't blame my
body-losses on the black city or briny Caribbean
night.

He says that's your problem-
the happy in your front teeth,
the way your purpl'd hips coil and flick,
it doesn't matter if you see themboys spirit
before body, themboys don't see
spirits and yes, babygirl:
they are looking at you.

He says what I should see first
is men-eyes and lusty sweat bundled
on men-foreheads and he says
if I wear shortskirtstightjeans and themboys
reach out and snatch me from red alleys,
that's on me. And by the way, he says,
if you don't bite hard enough
when they catch you, baby,
you're a fucking whore.

THE OTHER SAINTS OF NEW ORLEANS

The Tellers can read a soul, its dead colors and flashing heat. The Tellers can count your tomorrows. They sit at tables in front of Saint Louis Cathedral, with demon ash and devil bones, with divination decks and spheres of bleak crystal. They smell of old wine, horse shit and fresh spirits. They reach for me and anybody else, desperately. A streetwalker passes by and says, "If they really could see…they wouldn't be here…" but really, who could bear to hear an accurate future?

MY BLACKGIRL

Girl you so strong, you so straight up strong.
Look at them chipless teeth, at them horsemuscle legs,
look at that fatless face, with no wrinkle nor tear.

Girl, you got them blueberry lips that never
flip down, that hair crinkled like dark mother, hey
queen girl, goddess lady, my girl girl girl

I'm proud to call you My Girl. Talkin' bout...
Hey, how you get that michelle-mouth, that bey-bounce,
that rosa-ride, that tubman-tough, hey now,
you ain't like them weak-willed light girls, yeah,
you near man-strong. Hey Man-Girl,
you My Man, My Man, My BlackMangirl, hey, hey!

damnit, girl, you stronger than some man. Ima call you
Not-Man, yeah, you so special you ain't no man nor girl.
You so highup Ima call you goddess, so holy you
invisible, you just a goddess with no color. Damn it girl,
you so special, you just floatin' like Lord. Oh, baby, you
so angel nobody knows where you flyin',
Look at you! Just lookin' like holy nothing.
Ima call you Nothing, you goddess girl.
Ima call you Nothing, hey, Nothing. So holy
nobody can see you.

Hey Nothing! you so strong bet I could sass you
and you'd say uh-uh or gimme that twitchy neck,
like them black chics in the movies do, 'cause they
don't need no man uh-huh. Hey Nothing,
bet I could throw any rock at your blackface,
bet I could stick any thick thing in you, bet you so strong
I could push you 'round and you wouldn't feel my hands,
bet you'd just say give it to me baby,
like them booty girls do on BET.

Hey, hey, bet I could make you take any lash and
red would never appear on that black
skin, nah, you wouldn't wilt for nothing.

Hey Nothing Girl, you thrill me. I know you could
survive anyone, 'cause you so damn
strong.

Ain't you?

Hey, my BlackNothingGirl
why you whining for awhile, nah
that's not what magicblackgirls do.

girl look into this cameraface and dance like you got
fever, gimme them bullet eyes like blackgirls in bad pain
do, camon, camon

angryassblackgirl, bestrongforme be strong
don't feel nothing, please, so I can
test my strength with your beast will.

heyhey
be how I like you best.

Not as you are, now, where I found you:
in a little room, dirty, lonely, and
vexed.

that just ain't no fun,
blackgirl.

LADY'S NIGHT

I might have been roofied on
Bourbon Street and
they tell me I should have
remembered what happened
but I don't.

I do remember sitting in a jazz-blues joint,
on my last night in the Fattest City,
texting the folks of my life about loving them
fierce, 'cause when you're alone
in a jazz-blues joint in the Fattest City, you feel a
kick drum kind of rush, like somebody special is playing
a bassline just for you. That sound soaked me
in love and rhythm, in the kind of heaven you can't buy,
though I paid a few bucks for that cranberry vodka my
bouncer friend says only bad-tippin' black folks get,
but I'm black and the tip I gave this bartender was high
and generous, and about the time I was asking this bartender
how he'd put up this place, a blonde guy walked in,
wide-shouldered, young as a college boy.

The blondeboy nodded at the bartender and sat next to me,
said whatsagoodgirllikeyoudoingaloneintheQuarter
and I said taking a break from slave research for my book
about ex-slaves and he says that's nice I like this jazz,
and I said sure and turned away from him. I stood up
to clap for the band, then came back to my chair
and the blondeboy was near me, half-smirking
and he asked if my big breasts were real. I looked down
at my breasts, as if I suddenly realized they were big and mine
and these floppy knobs existed for real, and I said yes, dumbly, then
decided to leave him, because that's not a thing to ask a girl
so I took my cloudy drink with me.

Later, I found a new chair and sat next to the band. They
beamed at me, and I raised my hands to cheer for them.
Somebody I love texted me and said,
Thanksforallthenicethingsusaidhappy2knowu and
I sipped my drink, feeling happy I had somebodies who loved me,
and the bartender came over and said, heyyoumightwanttobecareful
ofthatoneguy

but his voice got gobbled up by Southern jazz and brassy blues,
and the band finished. I got up to clap and returned
to my first chair, by the bar, and started on my drink without
looking at it. I sipped it one more time, thinking about the warm,
love-feelings I was feeling for the folks who weren't there and
the blondeboy came back grinning and I was grinning too, happy
about my last night in the Fattest City. He put his face close to mine,
said, "I think you're very pretty," and I said, "I'm already taken,"
but he tried some bad joke about how I should be
untaken and I said something else but his face blacked fast and
I woke up in the bar bathroom with my bra off, pants and
panties half-pulled down, as if my vagina was considered
but rejected. I looked down and saw why—the period blood
staining the crotch of my jeans, I was already too bloody to take.
I saw my bare breasts, which were real but didn't feel so that night.
Those breasts felt gross and used up; they could have
belonged to another blackgirl that night,
or just somebody I didn't love.

I checked my pants pockets absently for my credit card,
and it was there, plus a slip of paper and hundred-dollar bill,
and I didn't know what made me more sick, looking at Franklin's
smug green face or reading the slip of paper that said,
you're cute call me for more research and I wondered if
the people I love would still love me. I wondered what
I had done wrong and when,
and how I was hurt.

I did not ring him but thought to call the police or Mami,
who had gone through This before Daddy loved her, who

63

knew about the time the other blondeboy tried this with me in
high school when I was trying to teach him trig, but I found my
shirt and put it back on, because I felt some kind of shame.
Because I thought maybe I shouldn't be in this Fat City alone,
as a black girl with big, real breasts and a dumb, big smile.
I thought maybe this is my fault for wanting solitude and jazz,
and I should have known that jazz is the Western African word
for sex, and drinking is English for drinking and men acting foul is
as natural as the cackle of night herons by bayou swamps,
so I ran out of the bar, just as the bartender saw me and
asked if I was okay but I was not,
so I kept running.

I kept running on Saint-named streets and ended up somewhere
I didn't recognize in the dark, somewhere
with bruised shotgun cottages, piss-wet trash and
sewer beasts gibbering but I didn't care about being lost,
because all kinds of dark felt the same.
I kept running, until I was past Congo Square
where slaves used to dance in circles before being sold
to Masters to sow, suckle and breed.

At some point, I stopped running.
I breathed in thick ancient heat and
listened to palmetto bugs cry and leaned my used body
against a bus stop sign. A man trudged up; he had a little
swagger. The man gave me a loud,
yellow grin and said: "Smile, pretty girl. It ain't that bad."

40 WAYS TO AVOID SEXUAL ASSAULT

1. Be alone, so you'll never have dangerous company.
2. Don't be alone, you need muscled protection.
3. Bring a man with you, women-friends attract suitors.
4. Don't bring any guy, just a boyfriend or male-pal.
5. Check: is your boyfriend angry?
6. Check: does your friend like you?

7. Don't look around, at anyone. Slap on sunglasses.
8. Don't put on sunglasses, men will want to fuck you.
9. Get very fat.
10. Don't get too fat, guys like fleshy girls.
11. Get thin. Be light-bodied so you can run fast.
12. Don't be too-thin, guys like twiggy legs.
13. Don't be tall either, you'll be easily seen.
14. Be leggy and long, you can spot the bad ones below you.
15. Be small and bird-like, you'll be quickly forgotten.
16. Don't be too little, someone might snatch you,
take you away.

17. Stay close to your uncles and fathers.
18. Check: Are your uncles and fathers kind?
19. Stay close to your mother.
20. Be careful of your mother, she might have a blind spot when it comes to you.
21. Don't go to parties.
22. Don't go to parties.
23. Don't drink.
24. Never drink.

25. Go shopping, that's where ladies act like ladies.
26. Don't go shopping, you might choose slutty clothes.
27. Go to school, you'll become an emasculating mate.
28. Don't go to school, that's where men groom you for love.

29. Avoid sidewalks, all the savages live there.
30. Drive everywhere you go, wherever that may be.

31. Don't drive anywhere, you might get followed.
32. Don't leave your house. Always be there, alone.
33. Never be in your house alone, someone will break in, steal everything.

34. Be ready.
35. Be innocent.
36. Be wise.

37. Find a large blanket. Make sure it is thick, wooly and wide.
38. Throw it on your body, the whole thing, nothing should be shown.
39. Hush, now. Disappear.
40. Repeat #39, until free.

POSSESSION

This is my body. Do not push it or smell it or lick it or press your hot nosetip into it. Do not knead or burn it; do not chamber or bleed it, do not stuff it or snatch it away. Do not press your cold you-ness into it. Not yet.

Because this is my body, treat it like holy wafer or sacred scroll. Treat it like something fragile and love-blessed and spirit-filled. Stay at safe distance when watching this body that smells of *platanos*, riverwater and cocoa butter curls. This body: a long future, its life-lines carved on brown wrinkles. This body: ugly and flimsy, slow-moving and brilliant, bulbous and misshapen.

Also, it is mine, mine
mine!

Don't touch my
fucking
body.

Not yet.
Because it is mine, this precious, tired thing.
Here are my requirements:
Request what you'd like. Accept answer.
Askaccept/ askaccept.

These are not rules for possession.
These are my only rules for love.

NOTHING AIN'T HISTORY

I am watching Cloverfield
Lane (the second one) which is a movie
about a girl who is deep-night
driving on Louisiana backroads
that sprawl and strain and disappear.
The girl is alone when John Goodman hits her car
with his rust-red pickup and she wakes alone
in John Goodman's sweaty bunker. He tells her
she should be grateful he has saved her, but
she is suddenly afraid of being alive.

While I watch the movie, I think about the week
before when I'd stopped at a Texaco for gas on
similar streets, somewhere on I-10, when
a Creole woman told me becarefulalonenowpretty
and she held my gaze long, and I told her yesyeahIwill
and Iloveithere but that last part soured in my mouth,
because Louisiana's swamprivers, white-sheet skies
and toffee women du Monde, throb with more history
and love than any chilly places I've lived before,
where nobody looked like me.
Still, I have never driven on roads so hidden
and bowel-black, so catacombed with American
past.

If you saw how dark those lampless streets could be,
you'd know how hard it is to only-love
highways that are flanked by long-pillared
plantations and Spanish moss hanging fat from live oak,
looking like elder beard, like shreds of slave clothes.
If you knew how chilling the voice of a whiteman
with a BlackRiflesMatter sticker can sound
when he sees you gassing your car alone, at a Texaco,
and says, hey beautifulwhereyougoinI'llfollowyouforsafety,

you'd know why that Cloverfield
girl was so scared.

I'll spoil the movie. The girl didn't get
killed by John Goodman. She did stay in the bunker
for a long time. You wonder if she'll ever find
a way out and she does. You think she is free,
but she has to fight these shadowy aliens
who thrash and claw at her from high sky
and prairie rookery. She beats all those aliens,
but the movie doesn't stop then.

Here is the ending:
There is no proper ending.
You don't see if the girl survives or not, you just know
she is somewhere driving and running,
driving and running,

until those Southern shadows catch up to her.

CRATAEGUS PUNCTATA

for Nina/Monica

don't
everybody know
about [Missouri
too]
goddam!

state of missouri, gotdamn!
little dixie, tellmenow:
with all this new-old history hollerin'
in suits like white sheets, tellme
what's your gotdamn state?
Daddy said he'd never
come back to you, nevernever,
said he'd spent his life
runnin' from your hawthorns
but here I am,
living on your land,
by degree'd coincidence,
my maytree roots, splayed and
straining in your
brown-white soil.

yo, state of Missouri,
state of my Daddy's Negro'd birth.
remember my Pops? Little and shining,
a black-drenched boy in first grade
he went steppin' into ivory elementary on
Delmar. First Negro boy in that high-stacked,
desegregated place. My Daddy
came to that St. Louis school for babies
and teacherlady said, on his first day:
Sorry we got to have this Negro here
but the state said we got to,
so let's just accommodate.

hey Missouri,
how you want me to
accommodate my love for you?
It's my second year amongst your thistles and
bindweeds, after feeling the farmblood
of your fatty cowpulse. When I drive through
the Lou on the way to meet some familyfolk
who remind me of hope,
I see grattifi'ed scrawl hollerin' fergusoninthisbitch and
maya angelou quotes about rising, quotes 'bout that darkboy
named Brown, who got gunned down on Canfield. You
tellin' me to forget Ferguson, to remember
you ain't all that bad and damn it I ain't saying you is
—all that bad—but let's not lie to our lying
brains about who you can be.

Lord have mercy on this land of mine! I don't belong
here I don't belong there!

when I grew up in the 'Burgh, Mami told me
stop counting the times you've been called
nigger or nigger girl or nigger bitch 'cause thinkin'
'bout all them countless times will sour your brain.
And they said nigger every other day to me
in that rich white district in PA, and I thought
when I crashed into womanhood,
I grew out of that word,
foolishly, but
now I am an adult in Missouri,
the land of my Daddy's Negro'd birth
and I've stopped counting the times again, Missouri.
Praire'd state of this reborn
United States, I'm a fullgrown girl
and your land is still callin' me nigger.

yeah, tellmetellme how you gonna swing, State?
Me and this freshmade family of teachers, lovers

and pals, we are crying listenlistenlistentous
from your country middle, but you are laughing
and bored, and tell us to preach to our choir, but
damn it ain't you the one telling us your rewritten
rules are God?
Missouri, State of our reborn United States,
the orange leader you rooted for
said on mid-day news, to the watching world,
that we, the leaders, teachers, lovers and pals
in this Missouri middle are disgusting/disgraceful,
and Missouri, land of my Daddy's birth,
you are so red this year, I can taste the blood
you are pleased to snatch and spill.

eyyo, Missouri.
First year here: students with fists
tight and pumping for protest
while black kids are singing
this is how they have hurt me at rallies.
Underpaid athletes are sayin'
we ain't gonna play your games so we sittin'
out, and some folks are sayin'
stop ruinin' our tradition we've always loved everyone,
as if they forgot James T. Scott, swinging off that
bridge on Providence and Stewart, when
townfolk hung him hard and
one-thousand folks—student and country—cried
crucify that raping nigger.

alabama's gotten me so upset
Tennessee made me lose my rest
but everybody know
about [Missouri too]…Goddam!
This is a show tune…
but the show hasn't been written for it, yet

showme, State.
what you want me to remember to feel good?

72

this: the sweetboy and lifepals who tell me,
when days get mean remember I remember you
or the kind-souled,
folks at your university who shout freedom in
big and small packs, who say we will help
you because with us there is love, or the rush of ecstasy
I feel when I see a class of blinking eyes, gobbling
up the words of writers they've never met
or the married men in Kansas City who gave me
butter pastries and a room for the weekend, and said
you're always welcome. You think
this is the ecstasy of you, state of Missouri, but you
will not get credit for our loves' love-labor.
see, my moments of happiness here
are not because of you. Oh, red
state of my Daddy's birth,
you are still negotiating
faux-hope, and while you do
we, your shadowed middle, your kicking
womb,
are finding hope, for real. We are
forcing it to the front,
bloodied and fresh, until it
sticks out. We are
showing you, state of Missouri,
state of this rewritten United States,
our new-looking
Crataegus punctata.

TO MONICA HAND

I wanted to speak
at your service,
woman-friend,
sing-cry your life
like a spiritual, but
Monica,
grinning sage,
Audre-priestess,
Nina-swinging song,
I had no idea
what to say, and God didn't
give me no spirit-words, just
old thoughts and wild,
active love.

today, I chant
something as holy
as hymn:

your name, your poetry,
those blackqueen spirituals,
I reciteyou to life

againagainagainagain
againagain.

DEAR HOMEPLACE

how boring
is your
ego that my
darkface
still bothers
you
this much?

/

In this country,
I have realized
two things, every
year, more than
before.

first: your politics
are not about me
and never should be

and

next:
your politics
are so much
about who I am,
I'm near-crippled by
steel-heavy
duty, the weight
of black-brown faces
that feel
like mine.

Damnit,
then.

might as
well use this
new-old body,
this red
beaten,
mouth
for
something.

THERE IS ALSO ROSA

Sometime ago, Cousin Ricky found out about my father.

Ricky lives close to where Daddy grew up, which is five minutes outside of Ferguson, Missouri. Ricky is sharp-brained, slick-tongued, and fought in the Iraq War. He was surprised Daddy became a famous doctor, especially since my father grew up true-poor and life-hurt. Ricky was impressed Daddy got out of the Lou and became an Important Man who makes kidney medicines you can find in every hospital. *McCauleys don't do shit*, Ricky said, *far as I know. Almost didn't believe it when Mama told me your Daddy was a doctor.*

Ricky does not have my father's last name. He told me he thought the McCauley name was plagued with prisonbars, drug trouble and liver sickness. To him, McCauley meant failure, a bad fate. But here was my Daddy: one of those bad-named folks. Acting smart and doing good with that no-good last name.

I understand this thing Ricky said, because I always thought my last name was no-good. Unlike Ricky, I never knew a McCauley outside of Daddy and my brother Tim. I didn't like McCauley for different reasons. I simply wanted a last name that fit my Blatina-black skin, something like: Marisol King or Kenya Gonzales or Magarita Freedman, a name that showed my ancestors had some kind of agency; a name that offered no dark surprise when I came into a room. I didn't know how to be proud of my last name, but I wanted to be.

Sometime ago, when I was a teen-kid, I found out about Rosa.

I discovered Rosa Parks's maiden name was McCauley. I found this thing out while working on a project for 7th grade social studies. I got a book about Black Heroes with Rosa's name on the first page. That name, in big golden scrawl: Rosa Louise McCauley Parks. I stared at the McCauley, loud and long, between the delicate-sounding Louise and the stately Parks. I thought then: could Rosa be one of ours? Was she, even superficially, part of me?

A year later, Grandmama let it out at a family party in St. Louis: she knew 'bout Auntie Rosa, said she was our kin. She was my greatgreatgreat grandcousin.

When I learned all of this, I thought my name wasn't so bad. Hey, a holy dark woman on a history-bus shared my blood-line. She'd spent her full, young life walking around Alabama with our ill-fitting name.

/

I am an adult, in Montgomery, Rosa Parks's homecity. Montgomery is clean, old-feeling and normal. Many folks claim Rosa's blood here; they are proud and confused and searching for heritage, like me. I say my last name to the folks who work at her museum and they say oh wow. Like it means something. Like it's a good name that doesn't belong to a Scottish whitegirl. Like it's a name that fits my skin. They say: Well, you're part of some legacy, aren't you? You should be proud. I think of my Daddy, Timothy, my Mami, my Georgian cousin Dee, Ricky and his Mama too. I say YeahIam.

I am an adult, in Montgomery, at the Rosa Parks Museum. I am sitting on a big fake bus, and going back in time via digital presentation. There is all this rainbow flashing and it stops on Rosa's face. I know this picture. There are only three or four photographs of Rosa Parks you'll usually see on television or in books. What Rosa looks like: calm-faced, fair-skinned. In that picture she is straight-backed, ready, pleasant, about to turn history into revolution.

There is a presentation in Rosa's Museum that takes you on Cleveland Avenue on December 1st 1955, when the Alabama night got cool, purple-red, shaggy with fog. They show us digital Rosa: she is dark-eyed and dead-tired, waiting for this historical bus to take her home. Rosa sits in her hard, famous seat and the night gets full-black. Her busmates are grumbling, the museum shows the other passengers—black and white—getting mad she's holding up the ride. She stares out of a bus-window while the bus driver barks for her to get up. She doesn't. Everyone on the bus is annoyed and yelling. The driver says he'll get authorities if she didn't move, and Rosa says, firmly, near-politely, "You may do that."

Rosa, you know, wasn't always-polite. You'll never see pictures of her hollering, but you know she can get upset. Rosa Parks, you know, wasn't always a Negro

Saint; she was a woman who could get tired. She wanted folks to know she wasn't body-tired on that day, though. Her spirit had been kicked enough times it got hard from hurt. Then that hardness got steel-heavy, wouldn't let her move from that damn seat. She said: "The only tired I was, was tired of giving in." The video at the museum quotes her saying this too.

I think about when I was a little girl, friendless and bullied by a bevy of suburban white faces. I think about them coolly slinging "niggers" at my child-face, remember them theorizing my skin was brown because God didn't wash black folks. I remember a whiteboy I sort-of liked saying, "I can see you in private, but we can't go home 'cause Grandma lives there and she's racist." I remember the richboy who cornered me after class and asked what black girls taste like. I think of when I was at Trayvon and Mike Brown protests in Miami explaining to red-eyed critics why black folk lives matter. I remember being at the University of Missouri, the morning after the death threats on black students. I remember coming to work and seeing empty buildings and sidewalks and quads, save for a few dark faces, even though dark folks were the ones targeted. I remember the blackboys in front of the library who came up to me, asked to escort me to my car just in case someone started shooting. I remember asking them if they were scared of what had happened the night before. They said, "Nah. No way. We've seen worse. We got classes to go to."

I remember thinking, then, manoman, darkfolks can get so tired.

After Rosa got tired of giving in, she did That Great Thing. They show you it on the fake bus. How she kept sitting, until the cops showed up. She is staring forward; you can't read her thoughts. You think, maybe she is angry, maybe this soft-featured woman is boiling inside, but you won't see that anger because her lips are a straight line. She is barely blinking, her small body taut; she is preparing for a battle you can't see.

You know, just by looking at that face, you should watch out.

/

The museum presentation is over. I am talking to some folks who work at Troy, who knew Rosa. They say she was small, saintly, and kind. They are trying to find ways to talk about her like she is a real person while still being reverent. They are trying to say she wasn't all about that bus. They come back to the bus eventually, because how can you not?

They are talking about her as if she is an idea, not a person. They don't know how to go beyond her hagiography, but they want to. They try. They say Rosa was good at cooking. Her husband loved her; she loved her kin. I am wondering if this is how Ricky felt when somebody told him about Daddy being a doctor. Ricky didn't know anything about Daddy but he got proud quick. It was easy for him to talk about my father in symbols, as if my Daddy represented success and transcendence of stereotypes. I think of my own father the same way, resume-first.

This is a survival technique, for dark people: if your kin does good, you mention that good first. Everybody else will be trying to find some speck or thorn.

/

I am an adult, in Montgomery. I linger in the lobby of the museum. An elderly blackman walks in, goes straight past the front desk. He does not share Rosa's blood. He has lived in Montgomery all of his life, and came in the museum looking for a bathroom. The oldman can't find it. He approaches me and grumbles about the lack of obvious bathrooms. I say ohyeah, though I'm not in the mood to care about what he is talking about. He says, "You look like a young woman," as if he assumes I don't know what I look like. "Sure," I say. After being in antebellum South and researching Reconstruction for the past few weeks, this skin feels ancient, but he is right—I am nauseatingly young, in the scheme of things.

The oldman asks why I am here, in this place without obvious bathrooms. I say I admire Rosa and add quietly, as if I don't deserve to say it, she was related to my Grandfather. The oldman doesn't congratulate me. He tells me to remember Rosa was just another sweet-smiled woman who lived in his town. She wasn't just about busses and revolution. He says remember she was a woman too, like you. He means things I know but hadn't thought much about because I was so full of pride: That Rosa loved, got sad, was unhappy. That she had other sides too, not just what they show us in Negro Temples.

Then the oldman says: Man, I got to take a shit.

I try to help him find the bathroom, but he walks out quick, unsatisfied.

/

When I leave the museum, I see a gleaming statue of Rosa. I look at this Rosa, the not-real, frozen one encased in polished bronze. She is sitting serenely, looking off at something. You don't know what she is looking at. You can't know what she is staring at, this fake Rosa, and you'll never know what the real Rosa—the one they modeled this statue after—was looking at either. In this museum, at least, we are supposed to assume she is looking through a bus-window, forever.

I stare at her man-made eyes. Those eyes: defiant and aggressively calm. That look: lonely, tired of being slapped, resolved. Those eyes tell her body, a body warm with blood like mine: sit and rise on your own terms.

I've seen that look in my Daddy's eyes, in the eyes of so many dark folks who have not been awarded Negro Sainthood.

Their eyes: beat-up, steely and shining, looking forward to Something Important.

Jennifer Maritza McCauley is a writer, teacher, and Ph.D. candidate in creative writing at the University of Missouri. She has held or presently holds editorial positions at *The Missouri Review, Origins Literary Journal, Fjords Review, Sliver of Stone Magazine* and *The Florida Book Review*. She has received an Academy of American Poets University Award, and fellowships from Kimbilio, CantoMundo, Sundress Academy of the Arts, and the Knight Foundation, and her writing has been called a "Short Story of the Day" by *Seattle Review of Books* and "Poem of the Week" by *Split this Rock*. Her most recent work appears in *Passages North, Columbia Journal, The Los Angeles Review, Jabberwock Review, Puerto del Sol, A Shadow Map* (Civil Coping Mechanisms Press) and *The Feminist Wire* among other outlets.

https://jennifermaritzamccauley.wordpress.com

Lightning Source UK Ltd.
Milton Keynes UK
UKOW04f2345220917
309722UK00001B/153/P